Get a Grip!

This edition published in the UK in 2003 exclusively for

WHSmith Limited
Greenbridge Road
Swindon SN3 3LD
www.WHSmith.co.uk

Created by Essential Works
168a Camden Street
London NW1 9PT

A catalogue record for this book is available from the
British Library.

ISBN: 0 9545493 2 5

Printed and bound in Singapore

Get a Grip!

Hugh Templeman

POWER PLAY

It is thought that 14 of the last 17 US Presidents have been golfers, but few can have better credentials than the two Bush Presidents. One of George W's great grandfathers, Prescott Bush, was secretary of the USGA in the thirties, while another, George Herbert Walker, donated the International Challenge Trophy in 1921 that has since become known as The Walker Cup. Dubya may not be as keen a golfer as his predecessor, Bill Clinton, who could regularly be found on a golf course. Apparently it helped him to act like a regular guy. His idea of a normal person does seem curious – how many other regular guys are accompanied on a round by six golf carts, all carrying Secret Service Agents, a police sniper and a man armed with US Nuclear codes?

Golf is like the Presidential Election.
The guy with the highest score loses

FOOD FOR THOUGHT

In *How I Play Golf,* one of many books credited to him, Tiger Woods stresses the importance of a balanced diet. Apparently green vegetables, egg whites and rice all make him win, whereas cheesecake and gravy are strictly off the menu before a round. Yet when asked to select the menu for the 1998 Masters' Champions dinner, Woods offered cheeseburgers, French fries, and strawberry or vanilla shakes. Former Champion Byron Nelson was particularly pleased with the selection, explaining, 'This is the first hamburger I've had – my wife won't let me have one.' Not all of his fellow diners were impressed. 96-year-old Gene Sarazen complained 'Whoever heard of a cheeseburger as a dinner?'

More roughs than greens

Either way he's going to have a headache in the morning

IT'S MY ROUND

South African Ernie Els has recently started producing his own wine. The 2000 Engelbrecht-Els wine was released in 2002 and received the highest rating yet given to a South African wine. According to Els' official website the aim with the wine is 'to capture everything that Els stands for: big in stature and gentle in character.'

Winemaker Louis Strydom took the pretentious comments a whole stage further by gushing, 'Golf and wine show good synergies, as they are both heavily reliant on nature.'

Els is not the first golfer to launch his own wine, with Greg Norman, amongst others, also deciding that the synergies between golf and wine were good.

QUOTE UNQUOTE

66 **If you drink, don't drive. Don't even putt.** 99

Dean Martin.

TIGER, TIGER BURNING BRIGHT

Bob Williams at Burns Sports, a Chicago based sports marketing company, calculated that viewing figures in America for golf tournaments rise by 40 per cent if Tiger Woods is competing.

It is not just the TV companies that benefit from Tiger's success. Wood's New Zealand caddy, Steve Williams, is the highest paid sportsman among his countrymen. His earnings outrank even those of All Blacks rugby wing, Jonah Lomu, and Black Cap cricketer, Chris Cairns.

EVERY SECOND COUNTS

In 1986 Australian Greg Norman led all four Majors after three rounds, yet ended the season only winning The Open. In all, the Great White Shark has finished runner up eight times in Majors, most famously conceding a six shot lead to Nick Faldo on the final round of the 1996 Masters.

He is one of only two players (the other being Craig Wood in the thirties) to have lost in a play-off for all four Majors. Fuzzy Zoeller beat him in an 18-hole play-off in the US Open in 1984, Larry Mize denied him by chipping in at the 87 Masters. He then lost the play-off to Mark Calcavecchia at Troon in 1989 despite shooting a final round 64, and completed the unwanted set by losing the 1993 US PGA to Paul Azinger.

All the best golfers use their heads

NICKLAUS SILVER

Despite winning a staggering 18 Major titles during his career, Jack Nicklaus has actually finished runner up in Majors more often than he has won. Interestingly only one of his 19 runners-up positions came after a play-off – in the 1971 US Open to Lee Trevino.

No other player can claim more second places in The Open than Jack. On seven occasions he has found himself a runner up, and despite finishing in the top five on an incredible 16 occasions, he only won the tournament a relatively modest three times.

GOLF AND THE UNDER 60S

Annika Sorenstam's incredible second round score of 59 in the 2001 Standard Register Ping tournament began with eight straight birdies. Her 13 under par round followed her seven under par 65 on the first day. Her playing partners during the remarkable round were Meg Mallon and the defending champion, Charlotta Sorenstam, her sister.

The round of 59 beat her own lowest round record, which she shared with Karrie Webb and Se Ri Pak, by two shots. She ended the tournament with a modest 68 and 69 to finish 27 under par. It was more than enough to take the title.

IF YOU BREAK 35, WATCH YOUR COUNTRY

Annika Sorenstam's remarkable round of 59 has been matched by three men on the men's PGA. David Duval, Chip Beck, and Al Geiberger have all broken 60, although Shigeki Maruyama went one better, shooting 58, in the US Open qualifying round in 2000. However none of these players can match the fantastic scoring of the North Korean Leader, Kim Jong-Il, who went around his country's challenging 18-hole course in 34. His spectacular round included no fewer than five holes-in-one. Cynics might suggest that an element of liberal scorekeeping may have occurred, but loyal, and possibly terrified, North Korean officials were quick to verify their leader's remarkable claim.

QUOTE UNQUOTE

66 If you break 100, watch your golf. If you break 80, watch your business. 99

Joey Adams.

GET IN THE HOLE

By the age of three, Tiger Woods had already managed to go round nine holes in 48. He had also putted against Bob Hope on the Mike Douglas Show, yet he had not matched the feat of Michael Hollis, who achieved a 50-yard hole-in-one when only two years and 11 months old. Future British Ryder Cup star Peter Townsend, managed two aces in one round when he was only 14.

The greatest number of holes-in-one in a season is said to be 11, by J Boydston of California in 1962. Amateur Norman Manley's 47 aces is said to be a career record, but for many professionals, a career can pass without that one magical moment. Harry Vardon, winner of a record six Opens, only ever hit one hole-in-one, as did the great Walter Hagen. Still, one is better than none.

I'm a lumber jack and I'm OK

OUT OF BOUNDS, OUT OF POCKET

Many spectators have paid good money to watch top professionals compete, but Argentinean pro Roberto de Vicenzo had the rare distinction of paying to watch himself during the 1965 World Cup in Madrid. Having hooked his shot spectacularly out of bounds, de Vicenzo trekked off to try and find his ball. He returned a short while later, but was now told in no uncertain terms by the nearest official that he was not allowed back in. De Vicenzo pleaded his innocence, waving the ball in question, but unfortunately he was not recognised by any of the course officials. Not only had de Vicenzo sacrificed two shots and faced the humiliation of going unrecognised, but he also ended up buying a ticket in order to resume his round. On the plus side, he found the ball.

IT'S A LONG SHOT BUT...

Despite improved equipment the National Golf Foundation claimed in 2001 that the average golf handicap has not improved in the past twenty years. New equipment and massive driving does not necessarily help your game. In the 1992 Texas Open, Carl Hooper struck a drive that hit a cart path and rolled on for 787 yards. This may have been the longest professional drive, but it didn't help Hooper. It took him a four-iron and an eight-iron to rediscover the fairway, and he ended up with a double bogey six.

This is not the longest drive ever, as Nils Lied once drove 2,640 yards – in Antarctica. Once the shot was struck it continued to roll on the ice until someone eventually managed to retrieve it.

❝ His driving is unbelievable. I don't go that far on my holidays. ❞

Ian Baker Finch on John Daly.

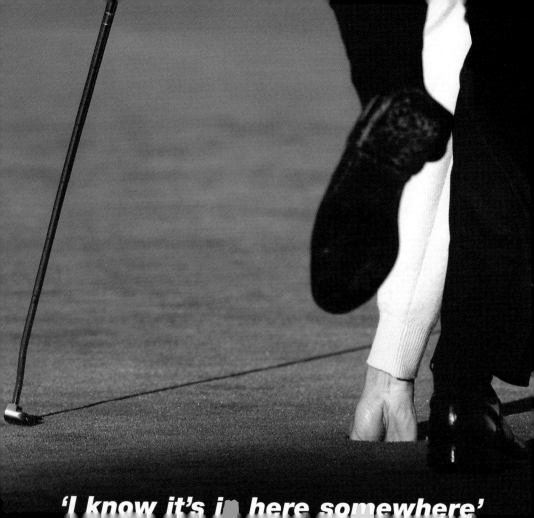

'I know it's in here somewhere'

JOHN 3:16

The Golfers Handbook quotes odds on a professional hitting a hole-in-one at 3,708-1, while for a standard hacker, the odds lengthen to 42,952-1. According to Golf Digest, the odds of making two holes-in-one in a round of golf are 67 million to one, which makes Rev. Harold Snider's achievement all the more impressive.

Snider had a round to remember at Ironwood, Arizona in 1976, picking up his first ace at the eighth. He then got two further holes-in-one in succession at the 13th and 14th. Three holes-in-one may be a record, although Kim Jong Il might disagree.

DID THE EARTH MOVE FOR YOU?

One of the more bizarre holes-in-one came in Mexico in 1932. According to *Golf Illustrated*, the golfer drove the ball within a few inches of the hole, and as he went to tap in his ball for an impressive two, an earthquake struck causing the ball to drop into the hole.

In the same year C.H. Calhoun and his son enjoyed their own impressive double. Playing a round together in New Zealand, they both aced the same hole. There were no doubt a few stories going around the Calhoun house for the next few years.

QUOTE UNQUOTE

❝ Man blames fate for other accidents but feels personally responsible for a hole-in-one. ❞

Martha Beckman.

FORE! FIVE! SIX! SEVEN!

For any standard hacker, it is refreshing to hear about professionals like Brian Barnes, who 12 putted the eighth hole in the 1968 French Open. He was within a metre of the hole after three putts, but missed two short putts and then picked up penalty shots by standing across the line of the putt and hitting the ball while moving.

Tom Weiskopf had a nightmare at the par 3 12th at Augusta in the 1980 Masters. Five balls found the water, as he scored a 13. Hermon Tissies at the 1950 Open at Troon took 15 shots at the 130 yard eighth, including five in one bunker. Ignacio Garrido hit a 15 at his first ever Masters in 1998. Tommy Armour can eclipse all with his 23 in the 1927 Shawnee Open.

221 REASONS TO GIVE UP GOLF

It is one thing to have a bad hole, but it is quite another to continue the horrendous run across 36 holes. Walter Danecki brought cheer to every social golfer in the world in 1965 when he entered The Open. The American started poorly in his first qualifying round and carded a whopping 108. Sadly for Danecki, things were not to improve in round two, as he stumbled to a 113. His total of 221 left him 81 over for the two rounds. He failed to qualify for The Open.

Even worse was the performance of Maurice Flitcroft during qualifying at Formby in 1976. Flitcroft completed a round in 121 but withdrew before the second round, explaining, 'I have no chance of qualifying.'

TEED OFF

Despite winning the US PGA as a wild card in 1991, and then claiming The Open title in 1995, John Daly is probably more famous for his ability to self-destruct. The big-hitting Daly has been plagued by problems on and off the course, and actually withdrew from the 1997 US Open after 27 holes, because he was shaking too much as he attempted to give up alcohol. In the 2000 US Open he took 14 on the final hole, finding a back yard and then the Pacific Ocean on three occasions. This wasn't even his worst hole – he took an 18 on the sixth at the Bay Hill Invitational in 1998, hitting the water six times. He came back two years later and hit an 87 in the final round.

QUOTE UNQUOTE

❝ It's hard to tell who's going to win this week, but it probably won't be a big, fat guy. ❞

David Feherty on the heat and humidity during the US PGA in 2001.

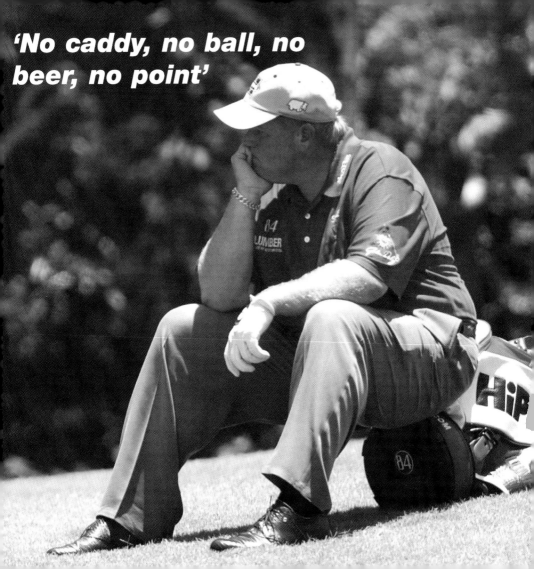

'No caddy, no ball, no beer, no point'

OW! THAT HURTS

Injuries on golf courses are not uncommon, but some are more spectacularly painful than others. Brett Ogle, facing a tricky shot during the 1990 Australian Open, swung wildly and must for a split second have been delighted with his clean connection. Unfortunately, he failed to avoid the nearby tree, and soon found his ball flying back towards him. Before he could shout 'Fore' or any other expletive, he found himself lying on the ground with a broken kneecap.

Richard Boxall broke his leg while driving from the ninth tee during the third round of the 1991 Open at Royal Birkdale. Boxall's injury was slightly more serious than that of Craig Wood in 1941, who strained his back when picking up his razor to shave before the final round of the US Open. Wood played in a truss, but still managed to win.

'First my dog left me...
now my ball'

ZERO TORRANCE

Sam Torrance has always found original ways to keep himself off the course, with 1993 perhaps the crowning year for Torrance injuries. He twisted his right shoulder the night before the Open at Sandwich, while watching TV. He managed to improve on this before the Murphy English Open when he sleepwalked into a large flowerpot.

Torrance's tale of woe did not end there. He had to sit out most of the Ryder Cup after he hurt his little toe driving off in a foursomes match. Many may argue that a little toe injury should not prevent you competing in one of the greatest sporting events in the calendar, but Torrance had little choice once the toe went septic overnight. Torrance wanted to watch the rest of the action on TV, but he was worried about twisting his shoulder again.

EXCUSE PLEASE

Injuries are often blamed by frustrated golfers for a poor round, but Colin Montgomerie put his disappointing score in the 1994 Hong Kong Open down to an allergy. Having shot a 76 in the first round, Monty explained to the waiting press that he was allergic to the smell of garlic and onions. The press, no doubt slightly confused, listened as Monty revealed that the fertiliser used to kill worms around the course, smelt of both and made the big Scot feel sick. The press were not entirely sympathetic, and placed this ailment on their growing list of Monty excuses.

QUOTE UNQUOTE

66 **To be truthful, I think golfers are overpaid. It's unreal, and I have trouble dealing with the guilt sometimes.** 99

Colin Montgomerie.

Onions make
Monty cry

JUST A LITTLE PRICK

Anyone that is human has got frustrated on the golf course, but not every player has taken their frustration out on a cactus. Ivan Gantz, a club pro from Indiana, who played part time on the PGA tour, was famed for his outbursts. After one particularly disappointing approach shot, he actually jumped into a nearby cactus.

Gantz earned the nickname of Ivan the Terrible after a string of these entertaining (and often painful) outbursts. When on one occasion he scuffed a chip, he punished himself by punching himself in the face. A missed putt once led to Gantz striking himself in the forehead with his club. If his ball disappeared into the rough, Gantz could usually be found banging his head against the nearest tree.

IF GOD WANTS TO PLAY THROUGH, LET HIM

The weather is a constant menace on the golf course. Players often carry on in rain, sleet or snow, refusing to sacrifice their round for a bit of indifferent weather. However lightning is a more dangerous proposition. According to Erin Barrett and Jack Mingo, 12 per cent of all lightning fatalities take place on the green.

One inventor, recognising the financial appeal of the golf market, has patented a new invention to reduce these figures. He proposes connecting a batch of electrically conductive ribbons from either the golf cart or umbrella that then hang to the ground so that the electricity will be made safe. Alternatively, you could head to the bar and wait for the storm to finish.

QUOTE UNQUOTE

66 If you're caught on a golf course during a storm and are afraid of lightning, hold up a one-iron. Not even God can hit a 1-iron. 99

Lee Trevino.

OH BUGGY!

Golf is not the safest spectator sport. During the American Express Championship at Mount Juliet, several spectators were injured in a golf buggy accident. Tiger Woods, leading going into the final round, prepared to tee off at the first, when a member of his staff lost control of his golf buggy and headed off towards the crowd. Woods had to delay his shot for several minutes while the buggy victims were checked.

Three people were carted off to the Accident and Emergency Unit of St. Luke's Hospital in Kilkenny, with one of them suffering a suspected broken ankle. Another spectator was examined for spinal injuries but eventually cleared. It is understood that the driver of the buggy had not been drinking.

Sometimes the tension is just too much

OFF THE WALL

Carlos Rodriguez also fell victim to the golf buggy. Rodriguez, a member of Sergio Garcia's management team, was crushed against a wall and knocked down by the buggy as it reversed into the steps of the clubhouse at Lytham, two days before the 2002 Open.

Garcia, hearing the screams, rushed from the putting green to comfort Rodriguez, before Garcia's mother, Consuela, accompanied the victim to Blackpool Victoria Hospital. Rodriguez eventually hobbled out with a broken ankle.

LIKE A BEAR'S WIFE WITH A SORE HEAD

Watching Darren Clarke can seriously damage your health. In the 2003 Smurfit Euro, Clarke managed to knock Tracey Leaney, the wife of his playing partner and US Open runner-up Stephen Leaney, to the ground with a wayward drive. To make matters worse for Clarke and the naturally concerned Leaney, Tracey was six months pregnant at the time.

Fortunately the injuries were not serious, but the incident brought back painful memories for Clarke. 'The last woman I hit on a golf course was Barbara Nicklaus, Jack's wife, in the Open Championship in 1993. My record is not very good but she was ok as well.'

DEATH OR GLORY

Golf is supposed to be a relaxing sport. One survey claimed that as many as 98 per cent of golfers believe that the sport relieves stress. However the findings of Japanese Sports doctor, Keizo Kogure, present a different picture. His research published in 1993 concluded that golf is eight times more likely to kill a man over 60 than jogging. His horror statistics continued, as he highlighted that around 5,000 people die on golf courses in Japan each year alone.

John Hopkins University and Wake Forest University conducted a further study, which advised golfers with heart trouble to either reduce the number of holes they play or to take a buggy – but then that can cause further problems (see page 48)!

QUOTE UNQUOTE

66 My worst day on the golf course still beats my best day in the office. 99

John Hallisey.

SHOW ME THE MONEY

For the very top golfers there is a lot of money to be made from golf, but for some players, scraping a living is not so easy. 1991 Open champion Ian Baker Finch suffered a horrible slump in form after his greatest triumph and failed to make any winnings from the 18 tournaments he entered in 1995. American player Becky Lawson played on the LPGA Tour for five years and in 88 tournaments she failed to make a cent. She finally won $283 when she avoided last place at the Rail Charity Classic in 1990.

However much money top players may make from golf, few will ever come close to the estimated fortune of the late Karsten Solheim. Solheim, the inventor of the Ping range of clubs, was estimated to be worth $450 million by 1993.

THE FIRST SHANK IS THE DEEPEST

Seve Ballesteros is famed for his erratic driving and superb recovery play. He became known as the car park champion after hitting his drive into the BBC car park at Lytham in 1979, before going on to win The Open. Ballesteros has won The Open three times, but after 27 consecutive Opens decided to pull out in 2002.

He had missed the last six cuts, but for fellow Spaniard Sergio Garcia, 'The Open without Seve is not an Open anymore. There is something missing.' Seve had a massive influence on Garcia, who became the first player born in the 1980s to win on the PGA tour, with a two stroke victory in the MasterCard Colonial in 2001.

BIRDIE, EAGLE, COW

Golf courses are dangerous places for animals. W.J. Robinson famously killed a cow with a golf ball at St. Margaret's at Cliffe in 1934, but this was nothing compared to the carnage caused in Sweden in 1993. A Swedish farmer sued the golf course adjoining her farm, claiming that several of her finest cows had died of blocked gaseous transfer after eating golf balls.

Animal deaths on golf courses are usually more dramatic. Anne Marie Pulli killed a duck with her approach to the ninth green in the LPGA Ping/Welchs Championship in Arizona. To make matters worse, her ball ended up in the water. Councillor Withes went one better (or worse) in 1951 by killing two starlings with one shot.

QUOTE UNQUOTE

66 **Obviously a deer on the fairway has seen you tee off before and knows that the safest place to be when you play off is right down the middle.** 99

Jackie Gleason.

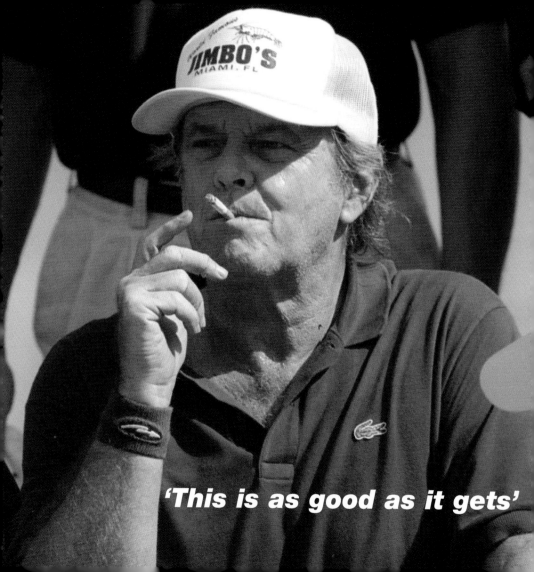

'This is as good as it gets'

BORN TO BE WILD

There are some golf clubs that actually make allowances for the wildlife on the course. A local rule at Bjorkliden Arctic Golf Klubb informs golfers, 'If a reindeer eats your ball, drop a new one where the incident occurred.' Even more worrying is the local rule at Jinga golf club in Uganda which states that 'On the green a ball lying in a hippo footmark may be lifted and placed not nearer the hole without penalty,' although whether you would want to hang around to replace the ball is a very different story.

A course in Arizona has a local rule saying that if your ball lands within a club length of a rattlesnake, you are allowed to move the ball. However, if you are within a club length of a rattlesnake you may want to move more than just your ball.

PLAY IT AS IT LIES

The South African Open was held up briefly in 1980 while a group of monkeys fought amongst themselves on the eighth tee. At Karen in Kenya, there is an encouraging sign advising quick action should a leopard appear on the course, while a sign at Marriott Hotel Golf Course in Orlando reads 'Do not feed the alligators.' Presumably these creatures live mainly on a diet of misdirected golf balls.

Slightly less dangerous are the crows that appear at Lithgow Golf Course in New South Wales. These birds still manage to cause chaos by disappearing into the air with golf balls. Imagine the frustration – a simple approach shot from the fairway becomes a tricky shot halfway up a tree.

BORN UNDER A GOOD SIGN

If you were born on 12 May 1970, you might want to take up golf. Incredibly, the first two Majors of 2003 were won by different players born on this auspicious day.

Mike Weir, the Canadian left-hander who won the Masters in 2003, was born in Sarnia, Ontario, while on the same day in Westchester, Pennsylvania, 2003 US Open winner Jim Furyk entered the world.

The odds against Scottish professional Andrew Coltart winning The Open at Sandwich in 2003 were slashed when a few sharp-eyed punters spotted his date of birth – 12 May 1970. However, Coltart failed to qualify and the surprise winner, Ben Curtis, was born on a completely different day.

'Darling, let's never part'

WILD THING

A number of golfers fancy themselves as musicians, but the big hitting John Daly has recently gone a step further and recorded a country album. The largely autobiographical album entitled *My Life* features guest performances by Darius Rucker, Willie Nelson, and Johnny Lee and, more interestingly, contains lyrics by Daly himself.

'It's a way that I can tell the fans how much I really love them. They can understand my life through these songs and it's really cool.' Apparently Daly has been a music fan throughout his life, and has collected 'almost 47 guitars from all of these great musicians and stuff.'

'And he's buying a fairway
to heaven'

REPLACE ALL DIVOTS

Golfers have always prided themselves on playing on in the face of adversity, and at no stage is this more tested than during war. Many courses in Kuwait were greatly affected by the Gulf War, yet still people played. Mines were found littering the rough, and one course did reluctantly lose six holes due to the emplacement of Patriot Missile batteries. 'A ball moved by enemy action may be replaced, or if lost or destroyed, a ball may be dropped not nearer the hole without penalty,' ran another local rule at Richmond Golf Club during the War. Note it does not explain what happens in the case of friendly fire.

❝ A player whose stroke is affected by the simultaneous explosion of a bomb may play another ball from the same place. Penalty one stroke. ❞

Local rule at Richmond Golf Club during the War.

SIGN HERE PLEASE

Irish Ryder Cup star Padraig Harrington is familiar with the runners-up spot. His second place in the 2003 Benson and Hedges International Open was already the 19th of his career. Yet Harrington's most painful memory from the tournament comes from the 2000 event, when he was disqualified shortly before beginning his final round. Harrington led by five shots, but was unable to continue after an official noticed that the Irishman had failed to sign his scorecard on the first day.

Harrington, who has an accountancy degree, should be used to filling out forms, but news of his disqualification filtered through less than half an hour before he was due to tee off. The £166,000 winners cheque ended up with José Maria Olazabal.

QUOTE UNQUOTE

66 Who cares about winning when you can be second? I love being runner-up. 99

Tom Weiskopf, being ironic (we think).

HOW NOT TO CLEAN YOUR BALL

A mistake from a caddy can prove very expensive – just ask Raymond Russell. Russell was in with a fantastic chance of a top ten finish in the 2001 Compass English Open when he approached the 17th green. Russell marked his ball, and casually tossed the ball to his caddy for cleaning. Unfortunately, his caddy misjudged the flight of the throw and both player and caddy could only look on in horror as the ball rolled gently towards the water. After a lengthy search in the water, Russell had to accept the ball was lost. He took a two stroke penalty and lost £4,500 in prize money.

OVERCLUBBING

Miles Byrne lived out every caddy's nightmare during the final round of The Open. Caddying for Ian Woosnam, Byrne realised on the second tee that there were 15 clubs in the bag, one more than is allowed. Woosnam had been testing two drivers on the range, and Byrne had absent-mindedly put both back in the bag. Woosnam immediately removed the other unused driver (by hurling it to the ground), but was still penalised two strokes, and was never able to recover.

The story of Byrne does not end here. Two weeks later the Irishman failed to show up for the final round of the Scandinavian Masters, and was promptly sacked. 'I gave him a chance. He had one warning. That was it,' was Woosnam's response.

SHOCK AND AWE

Caddying can be a dangerous business. Gerry Higginbotham, Sergio Garcia's American caddy, turned up at the German Masters in 1999 with two black eyes, a swollen jaw and six stitches in a head wound. Higginbotham was attacked in a bar, a few hours after the controversial American victory in the Ryder Cup at Brookline.

As Higginbotham explained, 'The guys didn't like the fact that as an American, I'd caddied for a European.' He ended up spending six hours in hospital on the Sunday night. However Gerry remained philosophical about the whole affair. 'It takes two to tango. I guess I should have walked away.'

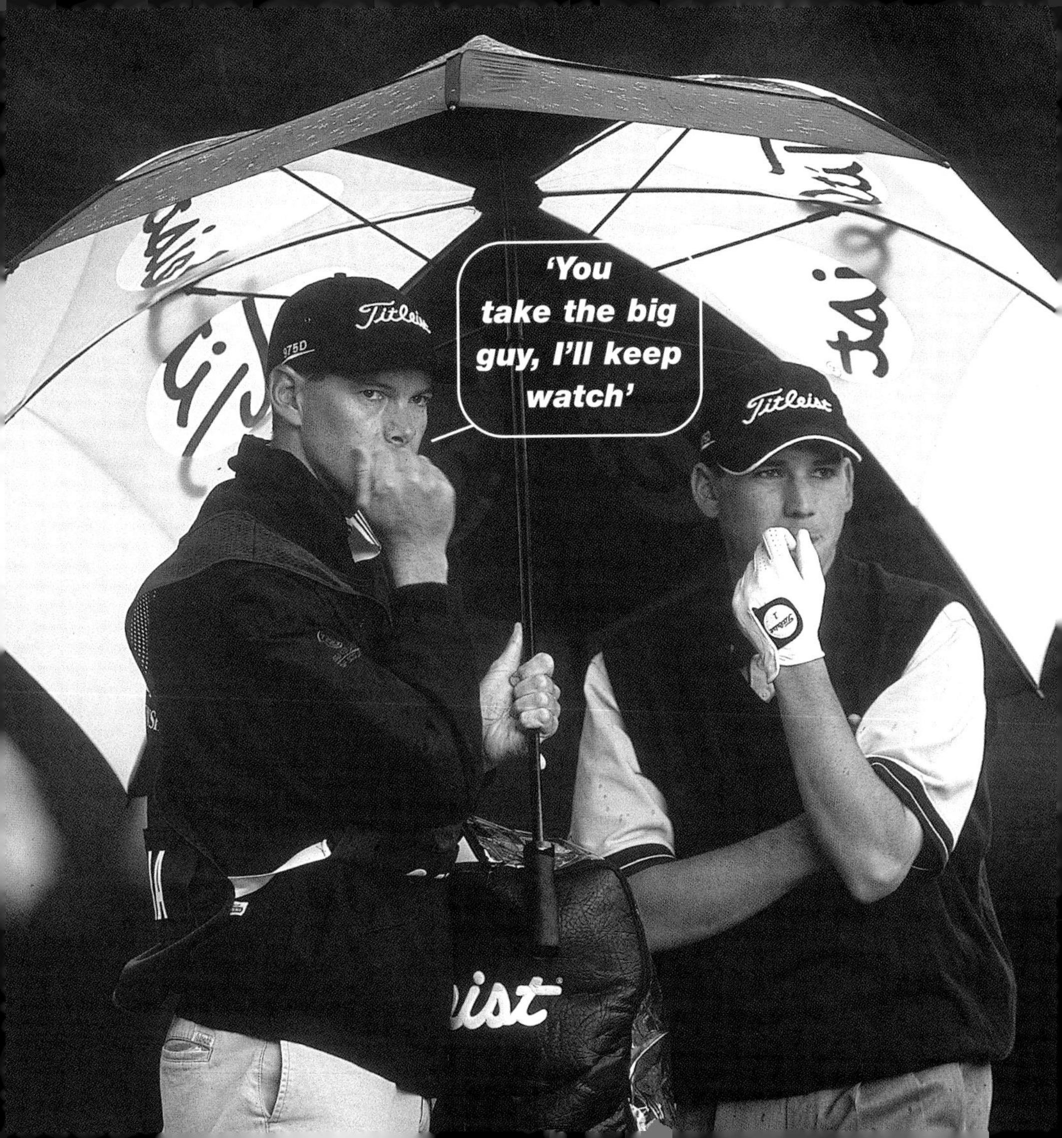
'You take the big guy, I'll keep watch'
Titleist
975D
Titleist

'Me and my teddy bear'

STAR OF THE FUTURE

2003 B&H International Open winner Paul Casey is one of the brightest prospects in the European game, having set a number of records as an amateur. The refreshingly relaxed Casey became one of only three players in 77 years to record four victories without defeat in a Walker Cup match, leading Britain and Ireland to victory in 1999. Casey also broke the scoring record previously held by Tiger Woods, when he won the 2000 Pac-10 Championship at Arizona State, finishing 23 under par.

He went on to become the first player to win three successive Pac-10 Championships, and also broke the ASU scoring average record, set by Phil Mickelson in 1991-2. Not a bad start to his career.

THE WORLD IS MY BUNKER

With improved transport and more courses, it is getting ever easier to play golf throughout the world, but the achievements of Ralph A. Kennedy are still worthy of note. Kennedy played almost 4,000 different golf courses during his life, claiming in 1950 to have played on half of the courses in the US. On a 24 day trip to Britain in 1951 he played 35 courses, including St. Andrews which was number 3000 in total. His record is all the more incredible when you consider that Kennedy did not start playing the game until he was 28.

Before Kennedy began his impressive tour, the record was thought to be held by the English actor Charles Fletcher, who had played on a mere 240 courses.

Course number 3000

AMATEUR DRAMATICS

When Justin Rose chipped in from the rough on the 18th hole in the 1998 Open he became a star overnight. His final round 69 left him joint third at Royal Birkdale, but Rose was unable to claim any of the large prize as he was competing as an amateur. This wasn't to last long. When asked when he was going to give up his amateur status, Rose replied 'Today, this moment.'

Jason Bohn came to the same decision in 1992. He scored a hole-in-one at a charity golf competition in Tuscaloosa, Alabama, and thus won a prize of $1 million. 19-year-old Bohn had to decide whether to retain his amateur status, or take the prize money on offer. It probably wasn't the most difficult decision of his life.

ALL THAT'S LEFT

Canada has more left-handed golfers than any country in the world, with an estimated 30 per cent of Canadians playing the game left-handed. The most famous example is the 2003 Masters champion Mike Weir, who is by nature right-handed. As with many Canadians, Weir played ice hockey as a kid, and so was equally adept at swinging the club both ways. When he was 13 he wrote to Jack Nicklaus and asked if he should switch to right-handed play. Nicklaus told him to stick with his natural swing.

Weir's victory in the Masters was the first Major win by a left-hander since Bob Charles won The Open in 1963. Behind Weir at Augusta was Len Mattiace, a left-hander by nature who plays right-handed, and Phil Mickelson, another left-handed golfer. Perhaps the lefties are on the rise.

FAMILY AFFAIRS

The early years of The Open were very much family affairs. The very first Open was won in October 1860 by Willie Park, who triumphed in a field of eight, over three rounds of Prestwick's 12-hole course. Park won again in 1873 when the famous claret jug was awarded for the first time. However he was not the only member of his family to triumph at The Open. Park's brother, Mungo, and his son, Willie junior also claimed victory.

Even more impressive are the achievements of the Morris family. In 1867, (old) Tom Morris won The Open at the age of 46, before surrendering the title the following year to his son, (young) Tom Morris, who was just 17. They remain the oldest and youngest ever winners of the world's most famous golf championship.

'Let's have a look at what you could have won'

PAR FOR THE COURSE

In the final round of the 1987 Open Championship at Muirfield, Nick Faldo parred every hole to claim his first Major title. This remarkably consistent performance was reminiscent of Gene Sarazen who won the US Masters play-off in 1935, by posting 24 consecutive pars. Sarazen parred holes 11 to 34, finishing the 36 hole play-off with 30 pars to beat Craig Wood.

Ben Hogan enjoyed 43 consecutive holes of par or better at Augusta in 1947, knocking in 35 pars and eight birdies from the 20th hole, as he began to establish himself as one of the game's true greats.

'Incredibly dull?
Me? In this outfit?'

IF YOU CAN'T STAND THE HEAT...

It is amazing what pressure can do to a golfer. Jean van de Velde's self destruction at Carnoustie in 1999, Scott Hoch's missed putt in the 1989 Masters, Greg Norman's tortured last round at Augusta in 1996 – they all show players crumbling under the spotlight.

After the second round of the 1929 Open, Leo Diegel held a two stroke lead on Walter Hagen. The flamboyant Hagen followed his usual routine and stayed up late in his hotel, enjoying a few drinks. As the evening became the morning, one of Hagen's accomplices suggested Hagen should think about sleep. 'Leo's been in bed a long time, Walter.' Hagen looked across at his friend dismissively, 'Yeah – but he isn't sleeping.' The next morning Diegel shot an 82.

THE WIT AND WISDOM OF...
LEE TREVINO

'There are two things that don't last long – dogs that chase cars and pros that putt for pars.'

'I really appreciate Lee Trevino Drive, its the only street in El Paso I can spell.'

'Columbus went around the world in 1492. That isn't a lot of strokes when you consider the course.'

'My swing is so bad I look like a caveman killing his lunch.'

'I'm not saying my golf game went bad, but if I grew tomatoes, they'd come up sliced.'

'I'm a golfaholic, no question about that. Counselling wouldn't help me. They'd have to put me in prison, and then I'd talk the warden into building a hole or two and teach him how to play.'

Asleep at the wheel

THE NAME GAME

The first lady golfer to be mentioned by name appears to have been Mary Queen of Scots, who was beheaded in 1587. Her enemies argued at her trial that she had shown indifference towards the fate of her husband, Lord Darnley, who was murdered at Kirk O'Field. They claimed that Mary had played golf in the fields behind Seton only a few days after his death.

Mrs Anne Sander has a particularly curious claim to golfing fame. Sander won four Major amateur titles, each under a different name. In 1958 she won the US Ladies as Miss Quast, by 1961 she had become Mrs Decker, before moving on to become Mrs Welts in 1963. By the time she won The British Ladies in 1980 she was known as Mrs Sander.

Phwoar!

CAN I PLAY THROUGH?

Golf is not famed for being a quick sport, yet Dick Kimbrough managed to complete a round on foot in 30 minutes and ten seconds at the 6,068 yard North Plate Course in Nebraska in 1972. The reason for Kimbrough's rush is unknown, but he completed a course using only a three iron.

Gerald Moxham of West Hill in Surrey won the Captain's Prize competition, after racing around his course in only 65 minutes to shoot his 71. Moxham had reluctantly attended a wedding and was still dressed in his morning suit. However none of these feats can match Ken Wildey who completed his round, with help from a motorised cart, in under 25 minutes. For some players it can take that long to find their tee shot!

'What's on ITV?'

'Has my wife gone yet?'

CAN I HAVE MY BALL BACK PLEASE?

A tee shot of over 40 miles is quite a claim, but one member of John O'Gaunt Club in Bedfordshire managed just this. A wayward drive landed in a passing vegetable lorry. The player could only shake his head as his ball disappeared down the motorway to London. The ball was discovered in Covent Garden after the cabbages were unloaded leaving the unlucky golfer with a very tricky second shot. A visiting player at the Eden Course, St. Andrews, was slightly luckier with his shot in 1955. Having sliced his shot horribly, the golfer watched as his ball sailed through an open window of the passenger compartment of a passing train. The ball was thrown back on the course, by a waving passenger, leaving him safely in the middle of the fairway.

QUOTE UNQUOTE

66 I'm like someone who built a fire but forgot to put a chimney in. I need a way to let the smoke out or I get very frustrated. 99

Darren Clarke.

'Same again,
but this time
hit the ball'

ROYAL...

Not all political figures are fans of golf. James II of Scotland, who ruled from 1437-1460, believed the game to be such a disruptive influence that he outlawed the sport. He felt that the appeal of golf was undermining archery practice, and that archery was likely to prove a more valuable skill when defending his country against the English.

Despite James II's efforts, golf has spread all over the world... and beyond. On February 7 1971 Capt. Alan Shepard, commander of the Apollo 14 mission, drove two balls on the moon. He struck both with a six iron (he didn't have a full bag to chose from), but had little chance of a hole-in-one, as the nearest green is approximately 240,000 miles from his tee on the moon.

PAIN RETIEF

2001 US Open Champion Retief Goosen has had to fight back from adversity throughout his career. As an amateur he was struck by lightning on the golf course, and he broke his left arm in a skiing accident prior to the 1999 season. He also became one of only eight defending champions in the last 50 years to miss the cut at the US Open in 2002.

However 2002 was a great year for Goosen, as he finished second in the Masters behind Tiger Woods, and finished top of the European Order of Merit. Alongside Ernie Els and the emerging Trevor Immelman, he has helped propel South African golf back into the spotlight. It is probably best to keep the skiing holidays on hold though.

'Ouch, there goes another hip'

...AND ANCIENT

Age does not need to be a barrier in golf, as 82-year-old Bernard Matthews proved. He comfortably shot under his age when he fired a 70 at Barnstead Downs club, while Arthur Thompson managed to equal his age when playing the 6,000 yard Uplands Golf Course in 103.

Comedian Bob Hope hit a hole-in-one at the age of 90, yet this is a modest achievement when compared to George Sehlbach from Florida who hit two holes-in-one in 1984 at the age of 97. Otto Bucher achieved his ace at the 130 yard 12th at the South Course at La Manga Club in Spain, when aged 99.

NO WIN, NO FEE

It appears to be getting increasingly difficult for amateurs to do well in Majors, and this is especially true in the US Open. Between 1990 and 2002 only 13 of 62 amateurs (22 per cent) made the cut, while only one, Matt Kuchar in 1998, has finished in the top 25. You have to go back 70 years to John Goodman to find the last amateur to win the US Open.

Even Tiger Woods was unable to challenge for a Major as an amateur, although he did make the cut on four of his six Major appearances before he turned professional in 1996. From then on he has hardly ever missed a cut.

'When I'm grown up, I'll buy my own shirts'

'If you beat me again, I'm stopping your pocket money'

LIKE FATHER, LIKE SON

Bill Haas was always likely to take up golf. The 21-year-old is the son of US Ryder Cup star, Jay Haas, with both men competing against each other in the 2003 US Open. Bill's uncle Jerry also played on the PGA tour, while his brother, Jay junior caddied for Jay senior at the 1999 PGA Championships and is a leading amateur on the golf team at Augusta State University.

And the family connections don't end there. Jay, who met his wife at a golf tournament, was introduced to the game by his uncle, Bob Goalby, who won the 1968 Masters, while his brother-in-law, Dillard Pruitt, played on the PGA tour and is now a rules official. However, 1953 Ryder Cup star Fred Haas is no relation.

QUOTE UNQUOTE

66 Give me golf clubs, fresh air and a beautiful partner, and you can keep the clubs and the fresh air. 99

Jack Benny.

DRESSED FOR SUCCESS

Jesper Parnevik is one of the more eccentric players on the tour, yet perhaps this is understandable as his father, Bo, is Sweden's most famous comedian. Parnevik, like the late Payne Stewart before him, is recognised for his distinctive golfing attire, yet he only began playing with the peak of his cap turned up because he wanted to catch a tan on his face while playing!

Parnevik is clearly golfing mad – he named his son Phoenix after the area in which he secured his first tour win – yet he has a bizarre mix of interests away from the game. These include magic, backgammon, yachting and perhaps most strangely, vitamins. Such is his interest in vitamins that his own company, Lifizz Inc. markets and distributes vitamins throughout the US.

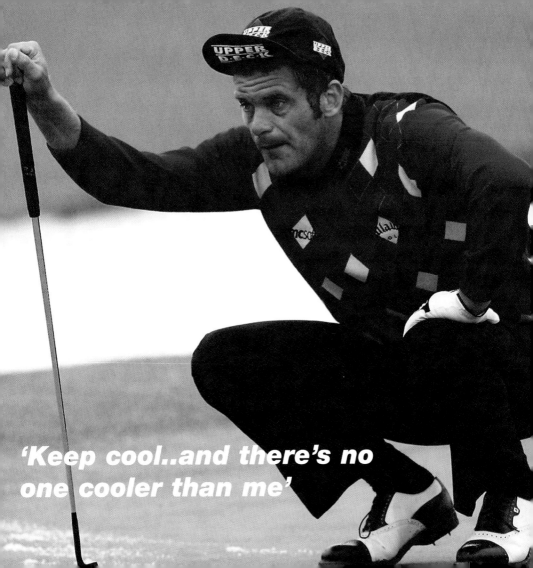

'Keep cool..and there's no one cooler than me'

STRIKE IT RICH

Rich Beem was definitely a surprise winner when he won the 2002 PGA Championship. Beem beat defending champion Tiger Woods by a single shot, and came from three shots behind leader Justin Leonard with an inspired final round 66, to claim his first Major.

It was a triumph of perseverance for Beem, who quit the game in 1995, and took up selling mobile phones and car stereos in Seattle. When he saw his friend J.P. Hayes win the 1998 Buick Classic he decided to have another go at the big time, and ended 2002 with season earnings of $2,938,365. More than the average mobile phone salesman picks up.

ONCE BITTEN

Andrew Raitt, a 33-year-old professional golfer, was so incensed by his deteriorating performance after being bitten on the little finger by a dog, that he went to the high court to claim damages of around £6 million for lost earnings. Raitt believed he would have been a Ryder Cup player, if he hadn't been bitten on the little finger by an Alsatian called Zomba, at St. George's Hill Golf Club, Weybridge, in June 1995.

Unfortunately for Raitt, the judge did not agree and awarded only £4,900 – all of which would be eaten up by the court costs. Raitt was left with nothing left to show for the incident, except a shortened little finger on his left hand. Furthermore he could no longer use Zomba as his grand excuse, with the judge explaining that the incident had no impact on Raitt's ability as a player.

GIRL POWER

Michelle Wie finished ninth in the 2003 Kraft Nabisco Championship. This top ten finish in the first women's Major of the year was especially impressive when you consider that Wie was only 13. She has since qualified for the US Women's Open, where four of the final six qualifiers were teenagers including 15-year-old Morgan Pressel, who was the youngest player ever to qualify for The Open, when she achieved this feat as a 13-year-old. Wie, who already drives around the 300 yard mark, has set her sights beyond the LPGA, and has already accepted an invitation to compete in the Albertson's Boise Open. This would make her the first woman to play on the Men's National Tour, following on from World number one Annika Sorenstam, who in 2003 became the first woman to play on the Men's PGA for 58 years.

'I'm stuck. Somebody
call a chiropractor'

DRIVE FOR SHOW PUTT FOR DOUGH

According to *Golf Digest*, tour players only hit seven fairways a round on average, and they only make 50 per cent of their six footers. However, occasionally a player will have a day when every shot hits the back of the hole. Kenny Knox had only 18 putts during one round of the 1989 Heritage Classic and used only 93 over the whole 72 holes, yet he cannot compete with Colin Collen-Smith who used just 14 putts in a round at Betchworth Park, Dorking in 1947. Collen-Smith chipped in on four occasions and single putted every other hole.

'What do you mean it's not a major?'

EASY RYDER

When Bernard Langer defeated Hal Sutton 4 and 3 in his Ryder Cup singles match at the Belfry in 2002, he must have felt a sense of déjà vu. Langer had defeated the same player on the same course 18 years earlier to help Europe to their first Ryder Cup win for 28 years. However on that occasion it had been by the slightly bigger margin of 5 and 4.

The star of the 2002 Ryder Cup was surely Colin Montgomerie, who equalled the best ever return by a European in the competition – 4½ points. José Maria Olazabal achieved that total in 1989, as did Seve Ballesteros in 1991, but Monty's record of being unbeaten in any of his six singles matches secures his place as one of the all time great Ryder Cup players.

EAT DRINK AND BE WESTWOOD

Lee Westwood is not the smallest player on the European tour, and has always enjoyed a good fry up, but even Lee has taken advice on his diet. Westwood consulted nutritionist Gill Horgan during the 2000 season to see if he could improve his fitness on the course. Unfortunately for Westwood this involved replacing bacon sandwiches with bananas and drowning himself in fluids and carbohydrates.

Westwood, like his great friend Darren Clarke, who owns a restaurant in Northern Ireland, is not renowned for his healthy lifestyle. He admitted that he strayed off the diet whenever he went near a restaurant, and the success of Westwood's diet is certainly open to debate.